Our Nation's Pride

The Pledge of Allegiance

By Amanda Doering Tourville

Illustrated by Todd Ouren

Content Consultant:
Richard Jensen, Ph.D.
Author, Scholar, and Historian

Visit us at www.abdopublishing.com

Printed in the United States.

Text by Amanda Doering Tourville
Illustrations by Todd Ouren
Edited by Patricia Stockland
Interior layout and design by Nicole Brecke
Cover design by Nicole Brecke

Library of Congress Cataloging-in-Publication Data
Doering Tourville, Amanda, 1980-
  The Pledge of Allegiance / Amanda Doering Tourville ; illustrated by Todd Ouren ; content consultant, Richard Jensen ; historical consultant, Magic Wagon.
     p. cm.
  Includes index.
  ISBN 978-1-60270-114-4
 1. Bellamy, Francis. Pledge of Allegiance to the Flag—History—Juvenile literature. 2. Bellamy, Francis. Pledge of Allegiance to the Flag—Juvenile literature. 3. Flags—United States—Juvenile literature. I. Ouren, Todd, ill. II. Title.
JC346.D64 2008
323.6'50973—dc22
                          2007034070

Table of Contents

Pledge to Our Flag
and Our Country

School has just started for the day. You and your

classmates stand. You face the flag and put your right

hand over your heart. You say the Pledge of Allegiance.

By saying the Pledge of Allegiance, you are showing

respect to the U.S. flag. You are promising to be loyal to

the United States.

Francis Bellamy and the *Youth's Companion*

The Pledge of Allegiance was written in 1892 by

Francis Bellamy. Francis worked at a magazine called

the *Youth's Companion*. It was a patriotic magazine.

Francis was also very patriotic. He wanted every

school to have a U.S. flag.

The Columbus Day Celebration

In 1892, the magazine decided to hold a celebration.

It was the 400-year anniversary of Columbus Day.

Americans celebrate Columbus Day as the day explorer

Christopher Columbus landed in America. The magazine

wanted every school in the United States to participate.

The *Youth's Companion* wrote a program for the celebration. Schools were to follow the program.

Part of the program was Francis's pledge to the flag.

This pledge became the Pledge of Allegiance.

On October 21, 1892, schools across the country celebrated Columbus Day. Students saluted the flag using Francis's pledge:

"I pledge allegiance to my Flag, and to the Republic for which it stands—one Nation—indivisible, with Liberty and Justice for all."

The Flag Salute in Schools

Many leaders liked the idea of saluting the flag.

Some states passed laws saying that schools must salute

the flag. Some schools used Francis's pledge. Some

schools used other flag salutes.

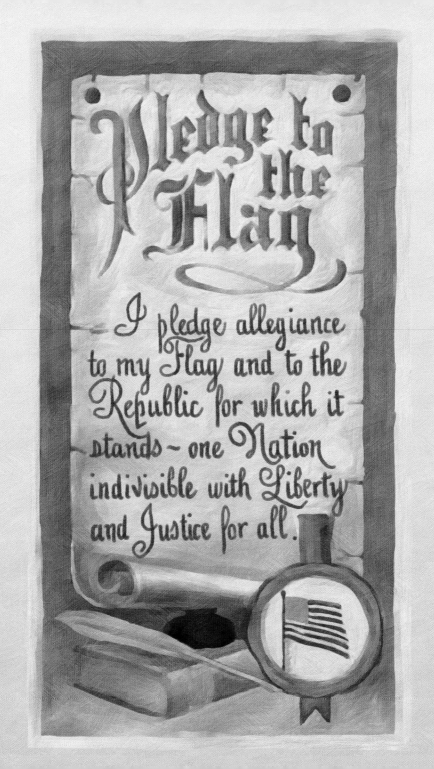

Francis Bellamy's Pledge

Francis's pledge is different than today's Pledge of Allegiance. It was only 23 words long. Today, the Pledge of Allegiance is 31 words long. Over the years, it has been changed and words have been added.

17

The Flag Code

In 1923, the National Flag Conference set up rules for the flag. These rules became the Flag Code. The Flag Code named Francis's Pledge of Allegiance the country's salute to the flag. It also told people how they should salute the flag. They should face the flag and place their right hands over their hearts.

Changes to the Pledge of Allegiance

The National Flag Conference changed the Pledge of Allegiance. It changed "my flag" to "the flag of the United States." A year later, it added "of America" to make it "the United States of America." In 1942, the Flag Code was made into law. The Pledge of Allegiance became the official way to salute the flag.

21

In 1954, President Dwight D. Eisenhower added to

the pledge. He added "under God," after "one Nation."

The Pledge of Allegiance became what it is today:

"I pledge allegiance to the Flag of the United

States of America, and to the Republic for

which it stands, one Nation, under God,

indivisible, with liberty and justice for all."

What Does the Pledge of Allegiance Mean?

Words	Meaning
I pledge allegiance to the Flag of the United States of America,	I promise to be loyal to the U.S. flag,
and to the Republic for which it stands,	and to the United States, which allows people to choose its leaders,
one Nation, under God,	and is one country under God's protection,
indivisible,	that cannot be split up,
with liberty and justice for all.	with freedom and fairness for all people.

25

When Do People Say the Pledge of Allegiance?

Many children say the Pledge of Allegiance every day at school. Lawmakers also say the Pledge of Allegiance at the start of each day when they meet. The Pledge of Allegiance is also a part of Flag Day celebrations.

26

Pledging Loyalty
to the United States

The Pledge of Allegiance was written for a

celebration in 1892. Fifty years later, Francis Bellamy's

words were made into law. We use Francis's words

to show respect to the flag. By saying the Pledge of

Allegiance, we promise to be true to the United States.

Fun Facts

• At least 35 states have laws that say schoolchildren must say the Pledge of Allegiance.

• Americans have not always agreed upon who wrote the Pledge of Allegiance. Many people thought Francis Bellamy's boss, James Upham, wrote the pledge. However, two studies point to Francis as the author.

• The Pledge of Allegiance was said for the first time in the U.S. Senate in 1999. Now, it is said every day that the Senate meets.

• Another popular flag salute was written by Colonel George Balch: "We give our heads and our hearts to God and our country: one country, one language, one Flag."

Glossary

anniversary—a date marking an important event.

companion—a guidebook.

lawmakers—people who make laws.

loyal—to be faithful to something or someone.

patriotic—showing love for one's country.

respect—to admire or honor something or someone.

salute—to honor or give a sign of respect.

On the Web

To learn more about the Pledge of Allegiance, visit ABDO Publishing Company on the World Wide Web at **www.abdopublishing.com**. Web sites about the Pledge of Allegiance are featured on our Book Links page. These links are routinely monitored and updated to provide the most current information available.

Index